W9-CLW-000

TOOLING AROUND

CRAFTY CREATURES
AND THE TOOLS THEY USE

Ellen Jackson

Illustrated by **Renné Benoit**

Charlesbridge

Tools help us everywhere,
on the earth and in the air.

Sewing, mowing, baling hay—
people use them every day.

Now and then you'll see a few
animals who use tools, too.

Among scientists there is no exact definition of a tool. But many scientists who study animal tool use define a tool as an object that an animal uses to accomplish a goal. Animals have been observed using tools to achieve objectives, such as obtaining food, attracting mates, protecting themselves, or concealing nests.

Finches with a cactus spine
dig for bugs on which to dine.

Woodpecker finches use cactus spines or twigs to dig grubs out of holes. They've also been observed scraping branches with pieces of tree bark in their search for hidden insects.

Hungry chimps have quite a trick:
catching termites with a stick.

Chimpanzees insert sticks, straw, or long blades of grass
into termite mounds. The termites cling to the inserted object.
Then the chimpanzee pulls the insects out of the mound and
enjoys a tasty termite meal!

Otters on an ocean swell
use a rock to crack a shell.

A sea otter gathers a rock from the ocean floor. Back at the surface, the otter places the rock on its chest and smashes a clam, abalone, or other shellfish against it until the shell opens. Then the otter dines on the mollusk found inside.

Crows that bend a piece of wire
learn to snag what they desire.

Betty, a New Caledonian crow living in a laboratory, was observed
bending a piece of wire into a hook, then using the hook to retrieve
a piece of meat from a tube.

Wild New Caledonian crows also make hooks out of forked twigs, which they further bend with their beak.

Here's a deer who's quite well dressed,
wearing grass to look his best.

Male red deer smear their antlers with mud or grass to appear bigger and fiercer to other males and more attractive to females.

Bowerbirds who want a mate
build and paint and decorate.

A male bowerbird builds a structure, or bower, to attract a female. Some types of bowerbirds, like the Vogelkop shown here, decorate with flowers and acorns. Others, like the satin and regent bowerbirds, coat a piece of bark or a twig with charcoal or fruit pulp and paint the walls of the bower.

Flies that want to mate—and live—
bring a gourmet gift to give.

A male empid fly presents a female fly with an insect wrapped in a cocoon. This "gift" not only entices the female to mate, but it also prevents the female from eating the male once mating is complete.

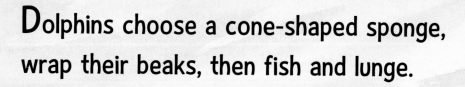
Dolphins choose a cone-shaped sponge,
wrap their beaks, then fish and lunge.

Some bottlenose dolphins wrap their beak in a marine sponge, either to protect this sensitive part of their body or to help them uncover buried fish on the sandy ocean floor.

Octopuses like to hide
in a shell—they're safe inside.

Veined octopuses have been observed carrying large coconut shells with their tentacles. These octopuses find coconut shells that have been thrown into the ocean by humans. They use the shells as a protective hiding place when they stop to rest in an exposed area.

Elephants of mighty size
swing a branch to swat some flies.

Elephants strip leaves from branches. They use the stripped branches to swat flies or other insects that bite them.

When a baby squirrel's at stake,
Mom kicks sand to scare a snake.

Rock squirrels build their nests in underground burrows. When a rock squirrel sees a rattlesnake, it defends its pups. The squirrel darts forward and kicks sand and rocks at the snake's head.

Animals must do their best
to find a mate or hide a nest.

When a human, bird, or beast
needs protection or a feast,

when there is a task to do—
tools will help us see it through.

Author's Note

In the past scientists believed that only humans make and use tools. But many now agree that humans share this ability with various animals.

What is a tool? Scientists don't agree on an exact definition of a tool or tool-using behavior. For the purposes of this book, I define a tool as an object that an animal or human uses or changes in some way in order to achieve a goal. For example, animals have been observed using tools to find food, attract a mate, or protect themselves or their young from harm.

Some tool use has been learned by animals in scientific settings. For example, ratlike degus were taught by scientists to use a rake to drag seeds through a fence. Some scientists would call this learned behavior tool use, while others would disagree. Crows have been known to create hooks not only by bending wires in laboratories, but by modifying twigs in the wild. Tool usage can sometimes be the result of human intervention, but often animals have altered items in their environment themselves to make the tools they need, showing their ability to problem solve on their own.

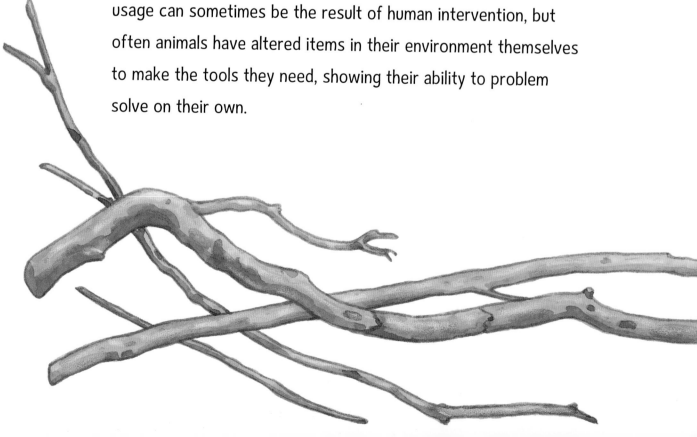

Are nests, hives, and dams tools? Most scientists call these constructions, not tools. But a few animals use tools to help build or decorate these structures. For example, when a male bowerbird "paints" its bower, the bark coated with charcoal or fruit pulp is a tool. Similarly, digger wasps use a stone to hammer pebbles and soil in place, so the stone becomes a tool, even though the nest is not.

Animals have found interesting uses for all kinds of objects, even those not usually thought of as tools. In one Japanese city New Caledonian crows drop walnuts on the street so the cars driving by can crack them. (American crows sometimes do this, too.) In this case, the cars are the tools.

For many years scientists have explored the differences between animal and human minds. While not all tool use is evidence of intelligence, we can now appreciate the richness of animals' lives and their ability to problem solve. And we can see that the gap between humans and animals is not as great as we once thought.

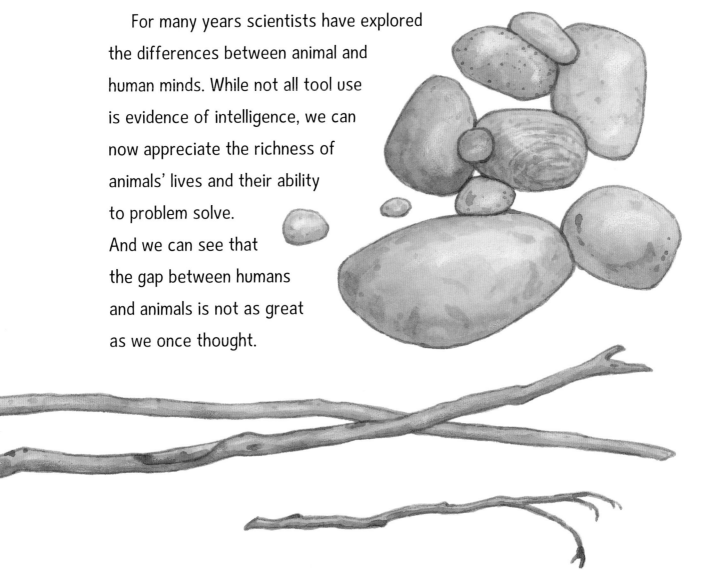

Where Do These Crafty Creatures Live?

- Woodpecker finches live on several islands in the Galápagos.
- Chimpanzees live in a variety of African habitats, including rain forests, open woodlands, bamboo and swamp forests, and open savannah.
- Sea otters are found in the Pacific Ocean off the coast of California, Washington, Alaska, Canada, Russia, and Japan.
- New Caledonian crows originally came from two islands in New Caledonia in the southwestern Pacific Ocean. They have since been introduced elsewhere.
- Red deer, sometimes called elk, can be found in Europe, Asia, North Africa, and North America.
- Bowerbirds live in New Guinea and Australia. The Vogelkop bowerbird depicted in this book lives on the Vogelkop Peninsula in Western New Guinea.
- Empid flies are found worldwide. The species shown in this book (*Hilara maura*) is common throughout Britain.
- Bottlenose dolphins live in warm ocean waters all over the world. In Australia they have been observed using a sponge on their nose.
- Veined octopuses can be found in tropical waters of the western Pacific Ocean and coastal waters of the Indian Ocean.
- African elephants roam throughout sub-Saharan Africa. Asian elephants live in South and Southeast Asia. An Asian elephant is depicted in this book.
- Rock squirrels range throughout Mexico and the southwestern United States.

Resources for Children

Books

Chinery, Michael. *Living in the Wild.* Leicester, UK: Anness, 2002.

Facklam, Margery. *What Does the Crow Know? The Mysteries of Animal Intelligence.* Layton, UT: Gibbs Smith, 2001.

Kaner, Etta. *Have You Ever Seen an Octopus with a Broom?* Toronto: Kids Can Press, 2009.

Patterson, Francine. *Koko's Kitten.* New York: Scholastic, 1987.

Pepperberg, Irene. *Alex & Me: How a Scientist and a Parrot Discovered a Hidden World of Animal Intelligence—and Formed a Deep Bond in the Process.* New York: Harper, 2008.

Websites

Inside the Animal Mind—Introduction | Nature | PBS

http://www.pbs.org/wnet/nature/episodes/inside-the-animal-mind/introduction/2081/

Information and videos about the minds of animals

The Learning Zone: Animals

http://www.oum.ox.ac.uk/thezone/animals/index.htm

Articles about animals and fossils from the Oxford Museum of Natural History

Think Tank Exhibit—National Zoo

http://nationalzoo.si.edu/animals/thinktank/

Thinking about thinking in animals from the Smithsonian National Zoological Park

Bibliography

Books

Griffin, Donald R. *Animal Minds: Beyond Cognition to Consciousness.* Chicago: University of Chicago Press, 2001.

Hauser, Marc D. *Wild Minds: What Animals Really Think.* New York: Holt, 2000.

Reader, Simon M., and Kevin N. Laland, eds. *Animal Innovation.* New York: Oxford University Press, 2003.

Shumaker, Robert W., Kristina R. Walkup, and Benjamin B. Beck. *Animal Tool Behavior: The Use and Manufacture of Tools by Animals.* Baltimore: Johns Hopkins University Press, 2011.

Websites

Animal Tool Use

http://www.pigeon.psy.tufts.edu/psych26/tools.html

A site with information about animal tool use, created by Lauren Kosseff in conjunction with professor Dr. Robert Cook, Tufts University, Medford, MA

NOVA | Tool-Using Animals

http://www.pbs.org/wgbh/nova/nature/tool-using-animals.html

Useful information and images portraying tool use by a variety of animals

Animal Minds—National Geographic Magazine

http://ngm.nationalgeographic.com/2008/03/animal-minds/virginia-morell-text

Photos, videos, and information on animal intelligence

To the Santa Barbara Wildlife Care Network, with appreciation—E. J.

For my parents, who taught me how to use so many tools—R. B.

Published by Charlesbridge
85 Main Street
Watertown, MA 02472
(617) 926-0329
www.charlesbridge.com

Library of Congress Cataloging-in-Publication Data
Jackson, Ellen, 1943–
    Tooling around: crafty creatures and the tools they use/Ellen Jackson; illustrated by Renné Benoit.
        pages cm
    ISBN 978-1-58089-564-4 (reinforced for library use)
    ISBN 978-1-58089-565-1 (softcover)
    ISBN 978-1-60734-751-4 (ebook)
    ISBN 978-1-60734-653-1 (ebook pdf)
1. Tool use in animals—Juvenile literature.
I. Benoit, Renné. II. Title.
QL785.J28 2014
591.5—dc23   2013014225

Printed in China
(hc) 10 9 8 7 6 5 4 3 2 1
(sc) 10 9 8 7 6 5 4 3 2 1

Illustrations done in watercolor, colored pencil, and
    goauche on hot-press paper
Display type and text type set in Humper
    by Typotheticals
Color separations by KHL Chroma Graphics, Singapore
Printed and bound February 2014 by Jade Productions
    in Heyuan, Guangdong, China
Production supervision by Brian G. Walker
Designed by Martha MacLeod Sikkema